D0969056

"There is an old proverb that says, 'Thoughts disentangle themselves when passing over the lips and through the finger tips.' The 17:18 Series which encourages us to actually write out the words of Scripture will be a tremendous tool in putting that proverb into action in our daily lives. I am happy to commend this project."

—Jerry Bridges, author of *The Pursuit of Holiness.*

"Rob Wynalda's The 17:18 Series encapsulates the biblical mandate to write Scripture on the tables of our hearts. By writing out Scripture ourselves and buttressing that with answering questions and taking notes about the texts, we will grow immensely in hiding the Word in our hearts and exemplifying it in our lives. This series of books is suitable for children and adults, for lay people and ministers, for Bible study classes and private devotions. Try a volume yourself. By the Spirit's grace, your soul will prosper, and you will want to write out the whole of Scripture."

—Dr. Joel R. Beeke, President, Puritan Reformed Theological Seminary, Grand Rapids

# The 17:18 Series

# The Book of
# Romans

This book belongs to:

_____

Given by: _____

Date: _____

REFORMATION
HERITAGE BOOKS

*Romans*
© 2009 by Full Quiver LLC
www.fullquiver5.com


Published by
**Reformation Heritage Books**
2965 Leonard St., NE
Grand Rapids, MI 49525
616-977-0599 / Fax 616-285-3246
e-mail: orders@heritagebooks.org
website: www.heritagebooks.org


ISBN 978-1-60178-076-8


Cover Design: Bethany Sanderson and Steve Coy
Journible™ Design: Rob Wynalda




Thanks to Josh and my WCBC Small Group

Why the 17:18 series?

Deuteronomy 17, Moses is leaving final instructions concerning the future of Israel. As a prophet of God, Moses foretells of when Israel will place a king over the nation (v. 14). In verses 16 & 17, he lists items that the king could not do as king. In verse 18, he transitions to what he should do as the king.

The king is commanded to not simply acquire a copy of the law (the entire book of Deuteronomy) from the "scroll publishing house," but to hand-write his own copy of the law. The purpose of such a copy written by his own hand was so that:
* he would read it
* he would learn to fear the Lord
* he would obey the commands of God
* his heart would not become proud
* he would not turn to the right or the left from following the law (Prov. 4:27)
* also, his sons would serve in the kingdom after him. (Deut. 17:19,20)

Thirty-four hundred years later, educators are "discovering" that students that physically write out their notes by hand have a much greater retention rate than simply hearing or visually reading the information. Apparently, God knew this to be true of the kings of Israel also.

From such understanding came the conception of this series of books.

Have a great time writing and learning the Word of God,

Bob Wynalda
Romans 1:16

# The Purpose of the Journible™

## Engagement:

The Journible™ is a profoundly simple attempt to aid a person's ability to engage the Word of God by slowing down the process of simply reading the text. The book is organized so that the "scribe" can slowly and thoughtfully engage the text while leaving plenty of room to write comments and questions about the text (Deuteronomy 17:18, Psalms 119, 2 Timothy 3:16,17).

## Legacy:

Journibles™ provide a legacy to pass on from one generation to the next. The Journible™ creates an opportunity for one generation to communicate in writing to the next generation their insights and personal applications of the text (Deuteronomy 6).

## How to use this book

This book is organized so that the scribe (you) will hand-write your very own copy of Romans. You will be writing the text of the Bible only on the right hand page of the book. This should make for easier writing and also allows ample space on the left page of your open text to write your own notes and comments. From time to time a question or word will be lightly printed on the left page; these questions are to aide in further study, but should not interfere with your own notes and comments. This means that you are encouraged to not only write your own "copy" of the Bible, but to also write your own notes concerning the text.

Yes, we are setting aside our mass-produced Gutenberg Bibles and attempting to get back to the simple hand-written copy of the text.

# Notes

Romans          ESV Text

Who is the author and to whom is he writing?

    The Apostle Paul to the Church in Rome

What was the purpose of the letter?




As you "scribe" the book of Romans, copy verses from
the book that you want to remember below.

# Notes

(1) What does it mean to be a servant?

Paul, a servant of Christ Jesus, called to be an apostle, set apart for the gospel of God,

which he promised beforehand through his prophets in the holy Scriptures,

concerning his Son, who was descended from David according to the flesh

and was declared to be the Son of God in power according to the Spirit of holiness by his resurrection from the dead, Jesus Christ our Lord,

through whom we have received grace and apostleship to bring about the obedience of faith for the sake of his name among all the nations,

including you who are called to belong to Jesus Christ,

To all those in Rome who are loved by God and called to be saints: Grace to you and peace from God our Father and the Lord Jesus Christ.

First, I thank my God through Jesus Christ for all of you, because your faith is proclaimed in all the world.

11

# Notes

Notes

(16) What is the "gospel"?

(18) Why is the "wrath" of God being revealed?

# Notes

(24) "Wherefore, Therefore" — why is this here?

2

3

4

5

6

7

# Notes

28

29

30

31

32

# Notes

(11) Why is this verse important to the original readers?

Notes

(15) Study and define Paul's usage of "conscience" in his writings.

4

5

6

7

8

9

0

Notes

(24) How can God's name be blasphemed?

(25-29) What was the purpose of circumcision?

1

2

3

4

5

6

# Notes

7

8

9

Notes

# Notes

(10-18) What are the attributes of man from this section
of quotes?

(23) What does it mean to "come short of the glory of God"?

9

0

1

2

3

4

# Notes

(25) Propitiation

5

6

7

8

9

# Notes

30

31

# Notes

(1) What is Paul proving in chapter 4 and what are the points he makes?

Notes

(9) What does credited or reckoned mean?

42

9

11

13

# Notes

(18,19) How did Abraham show his faith?

4

5

6

7

8

# Notes

9

0

1

2

3

4

5

# Notes

(1) "Therefore" — What is true in chapter 5 because of the previous discussion?

(3) See also James 1.

# Notes

(8) Memorize this verse.

(10) Reconciled

# Notes

# Notes

(18) Condemnation

(18) Righteousness

(18) Justification

8

9

0

1

# Notes

# Notes

(12) Therefore — Why should we not let sin reign?

Notes

(18) What does it mean to be a servant of righteousness?

Notes

(23) Memorize this verse and explain its meaning.

0

1

2

3

(1-6) What is the believer's relationship to the law?

(7) What is the benefit of the law?

5

5

(15) What is the problem in verse 15?

# Notes

6

7

8

9

0

1

2

3

# Notes

4

5

(1) Therefore — Why is this a great "therefore"?

(5-9) What is the struggle in these verses?

# Notes

# Notes

(14) What does it mean to be "led by the Spirit of God"

Romans 8:13-18

79

# Notes

# Notes

6

7

8

9

0

(36-39) What is so encouraging about these verses?

31

32

33

34

35

36

# Notes

37

38

39

# Notes

(1) What makes chapter 9 so great and yet so difficult?

# Notes

# Notes

16

17

18

19

20

21

Notes

(23) How should this make a believer feel?

2

3

4

5

6

7

Notes

(29) Review the story of Sodom and Gomorrah
(Gen. 18-19).

(31-33) What happened to Israel and why did it happen

96

28

29

30

32

33

(2) When is zeal dangerous?

# Notes

(13) What does it mean to call on the Lord?

(15) Are your feet beautiful to those around you? What is the historical context of this statement?

5

6

7

8

9

# Notes

(3) What is the background of Elijah's statement and what is the significance of God's response?

# Notes

(15-24) What is the lesson of grafted branches?

Romans 11:13-18

# Notes

9

0

1

2

3

4

# Notes

5

6

7

8

9

0

,

(33-36) What is the central teaching of these verses and how do they fit with the previous chapters?

32

33

34

35

36

# Notes

(1) Therefore — What transition takes place because of this therefore?

(2) What does "renewing the mind" mean and what type of things does Paul list that need a mind renewal?

# Notes

Notes

# Notes

Notes

(9,10) How do verses 9 and 10 relate to each other?

6

7

8

9

10

# Notes

# Notes

(1) Write a summary of this chapter.

Romans 14:1-6

# Notes

# Notes

1

5

6

7

8

9

10

(22) What is the warning of this verse?

21

22

23

# Notes

(2) How should this verse effect what you do today?

(4) What does Paul list as a benefit of Scripture?

# Notes

# Notes

1

5

6

7

8

9

Notes

‍

(31,32) What is Paul's prayer request?

7

8

9

0

4

2

3

# Notes

# Notes

# Notes

(17,18) Who are you to watch?  Why does Paul say this?

(19) What does simple or innocent mean?

7

2

9

2

3

# Notes

4

5

6

7

# Notes

# Notes

# Notes

# Notes

# Notes